COLOR & CRAFT
SCANDINAVIAN CHRISTMAS
Traditional Scandinavian Jul Designs on Keepsake Paper Crafts to Color

EASY PRE-PRINTED PAPER CRAFTS TO COLOR, CUT, GLUE AND MAKE
The Anni Arts coloring crafts are ready to color and craft in this book format.
'Print-on-demand' makes printing as environmentally friendly as printing the crafts at home.

KEEPSAKE PROJECTS TO COLOR AND MAKE: CARDS AND DÉCOR
ABOUT THE SCANDINAVIAN CHRISTMAS
EQUIPMENT GUIDE AND TIPS

GREETING CARDS
5" x 7"/*12.5 x 17.5cm* card toppers to color for art cards or to frame as reusable Jul décor
A MUG CARD AND TEA BAG: – This card can also be cut into the shape of the mug for a shaped postcard
FOUR JUL CARD TOPPERS in 5" x 7": – A Reindeer, Jul Goats, Tree with Folk Roses and a Christmas Heart
ONE FOLK ROSE CARD TOPPER in 4" x 6": – Feel free to add pink to the reds and greens
Download free blank templates to print as card bases at Anni Arts https://www.anniarts.com/scandi-clip-art.html

DÉCOR
FOUR LARGE ANIMAL PICTURES TO LAVISHLY COLOR AND FRAME: – *Jul Goat, Reindeer, Elk and Folk Horse*
SIX FESTIVE BUNTING/FLAGS/PENNANTS: – *To color and use as keepsake décor on a wall or over a door or window. Store the bunting in a large envelope to protect them for many years of Christmas displays.*
TIE-ON BOTTLE LABEL: – *Flying reindeer and tree. This can be laminated and cut to shape for repeated use.*
CHRISTMAS STOCKINGS: – *Use them year after year. Fill with candy, money or a gift card.*
TAGS: – *Double-layered to get the thickness for tags. Glue, cut when dry. Punch a hole for the tag.*

TREE ORNAMENT
Color, then cut beyond outline.
Score, glue, fold double.
- Trim after gue has dried.
Punch hole for
ribbon or string.

BONUS DOWNLOADS FOR PRINTABLE COLOR AND CRAFT PROJECTS
Go to **Anni Arts** *https://www.anniarts.com/scandinavian-christmas.html*
Red-and-white Gingham Paper *to wrap small gifts or to use as a frame background for the colored animals* ; Blank Templates *for card bases;* Tags; Bookmark; Coloring Extras *for card toppers or shaped tags of leaping reindeer and heart.*
More printable craft freebies of all kinds can be downloaded from **Anni Arts Crafts**
https://www.anniartscrafts.com/anni-arts-crafts-freebies.html

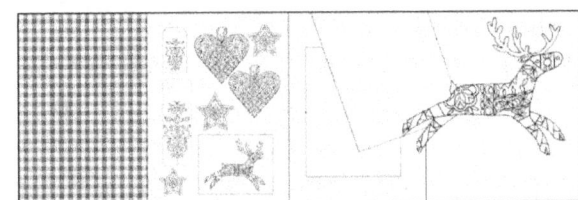

OTHER SCANDINAVIAN CHRISTMAS PRODUCTS
See the coordinating *Scandinavian Christmas Cut-N-Make Book* with pre-printed paper crafts in traditional folk *Jul* colors. The items are ready to cut, make and glue for cards, packs and décor.

The *Scandinavian Christmas* designs are also on the printable Anni Arts Paper Crafts and on a craft USB at Anni Arts Crafts **www.anniartscrafts.com**
The USB in a smart hard case makes a fabulous gift for crafters and lovers of Scandinavian folk designs.

And ready-to-buy *Jul* products like mugs, stockings, cards, packs, totes and more for Christmas celebrations, wishes and gifts are in the Anni Arts Zazzle store.
Follow links from the book's page on Anni Arts. **www.anniarts.com**

Text, Book Layout, Cover, Illustrations and Crafts by Anneke Lipsanen.
Copyright Anneke Lipsanen. All Rights Reserved. No part of this publication may be reproduced, or transmitted in any form without prior written permission from Anneke Lipsanen. Paperback Edition 2021

© ANNI ARTS

© ANNI ARTS

© ANNI ARTS

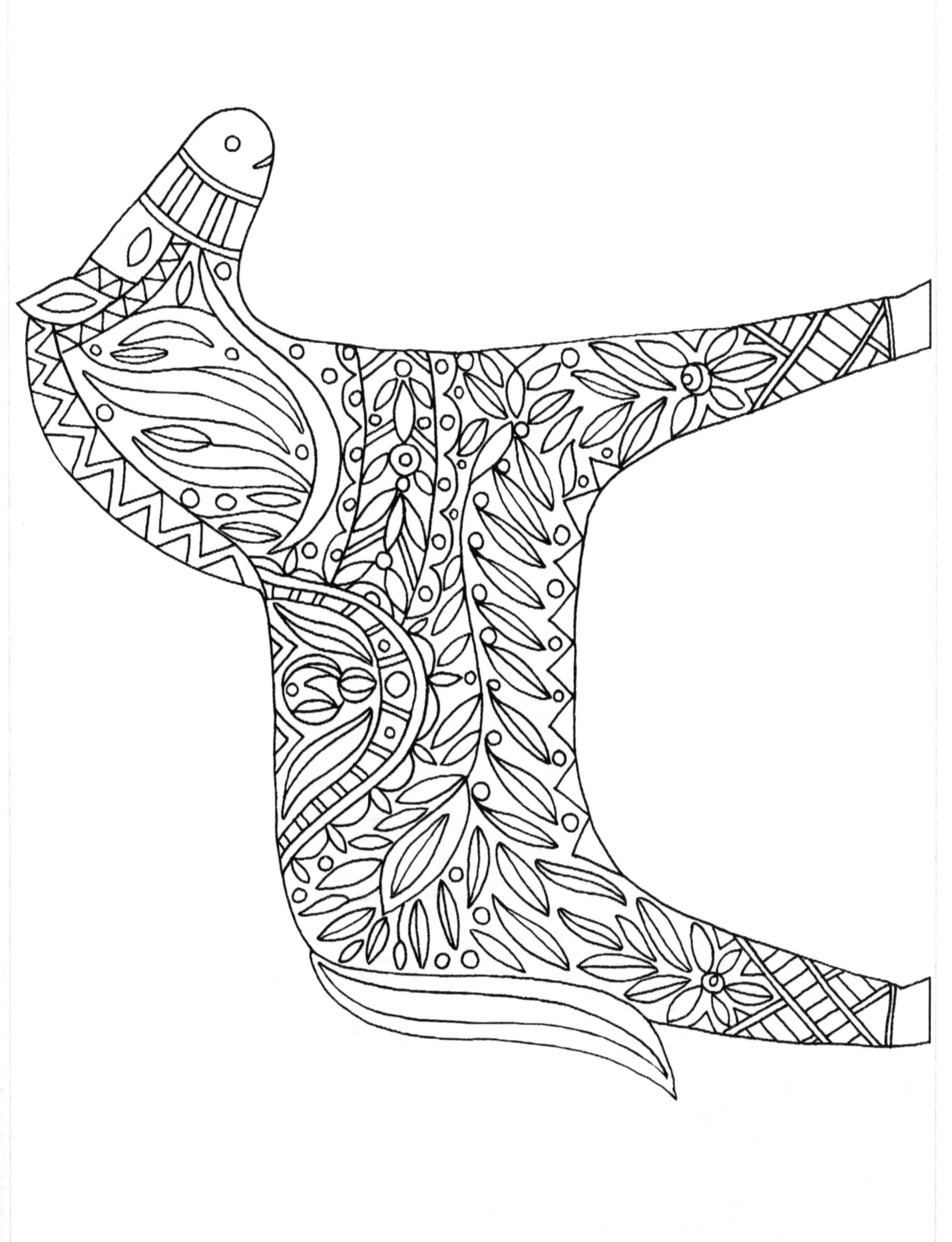

© ANNI ARTS

Score lines

MUG CARD TOPPER AND TEABAG ENVELOPE
Score gray lines and fold. Glue side tab and bottom tab to make packet.
Place teabag in packet, place tea bag string through top and glue and close top.
TIP: Shake tea leaves in tea bag to distibute evenly before placing in packet.

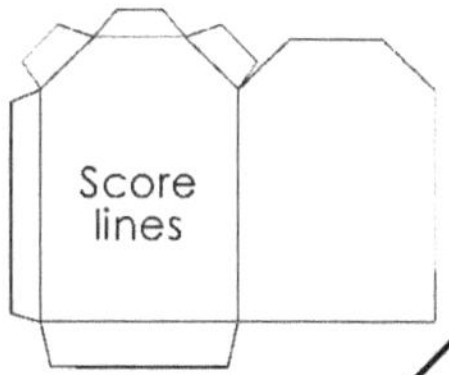

Punch hole

Cut just inside outlines.

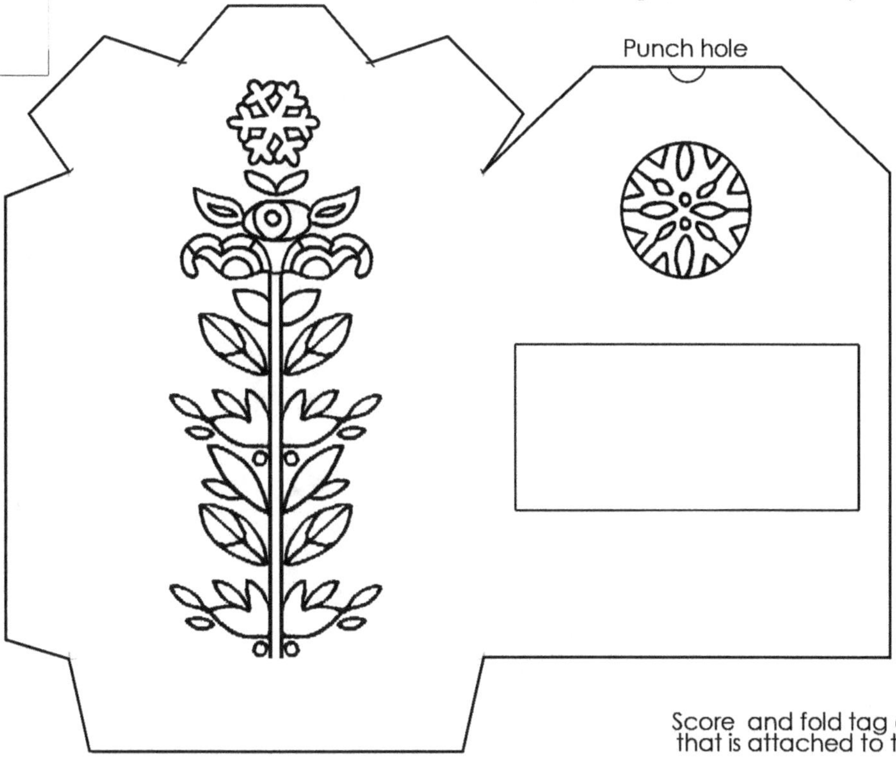

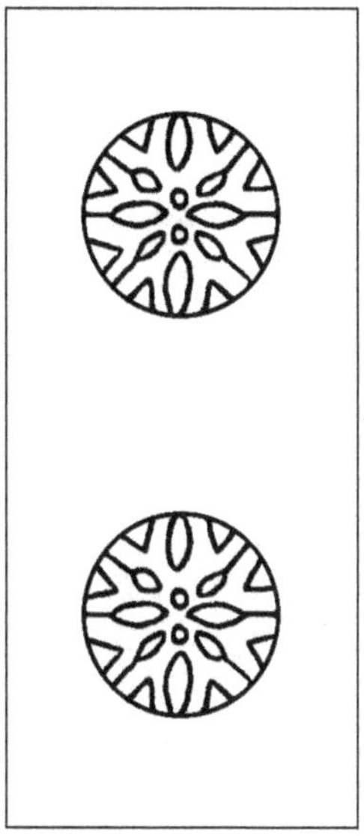

Score and fold tag and glue over the tea tag
that is attached to the teabag you are using.

All coloring pages and crafts are for private use and personal gift-giving only. No commercial rights included. No selling

Color and glue the topper to the front of a folded cardstock base. Glue the teabag to the inside for a nice little gift.
The mug card can also be shape-cut for a shaped postcard. Attach the teabag to the back.

© ANNI ARTS

CARD TOPPERS: REINDEER AND TREE WITH FOLK ROSES. Color pics and background (optional). Cut entire rectangular background and glue to a cardstock card.

© ANNI ARTS

CARD TOPPERS: JUL GOATS AND HEART WITH FOLK ROSES. Color pics and background (optional). Cut entire rectangular background and glue to a cardstock card.

GOD JUL
GOOD YULE

© ANNI ARTS

TIE-ON WINE LABEL AND 4"x 6" CARD TOPPER
Label with side reinforcement tabs.
Score grey lines. Fold all flaps back. Glue **under-side** of flaps

Punch holes in corner tabs once tabs have been folded back and glued. Thread ribbon through holes. Tie around a wine bottle.

FOLK ROSES 4"x 6" CARD TOPPER

© ANNI ARTS

© ANNI ARTS

DECOR STOCKING 2 FRONT
OR GIFT PACKET FOR SMALL GIFT
Cut on outline.
Glue to stocking back with glue applied to grey lines of back section of stocking.
Trim as needed when dry.

STAR DECORATION
Score as indicated. Cut on outline.
Fold. Glue well up to the edges on inside of star. Trim outline shape as needed.

© ANNI ARTS

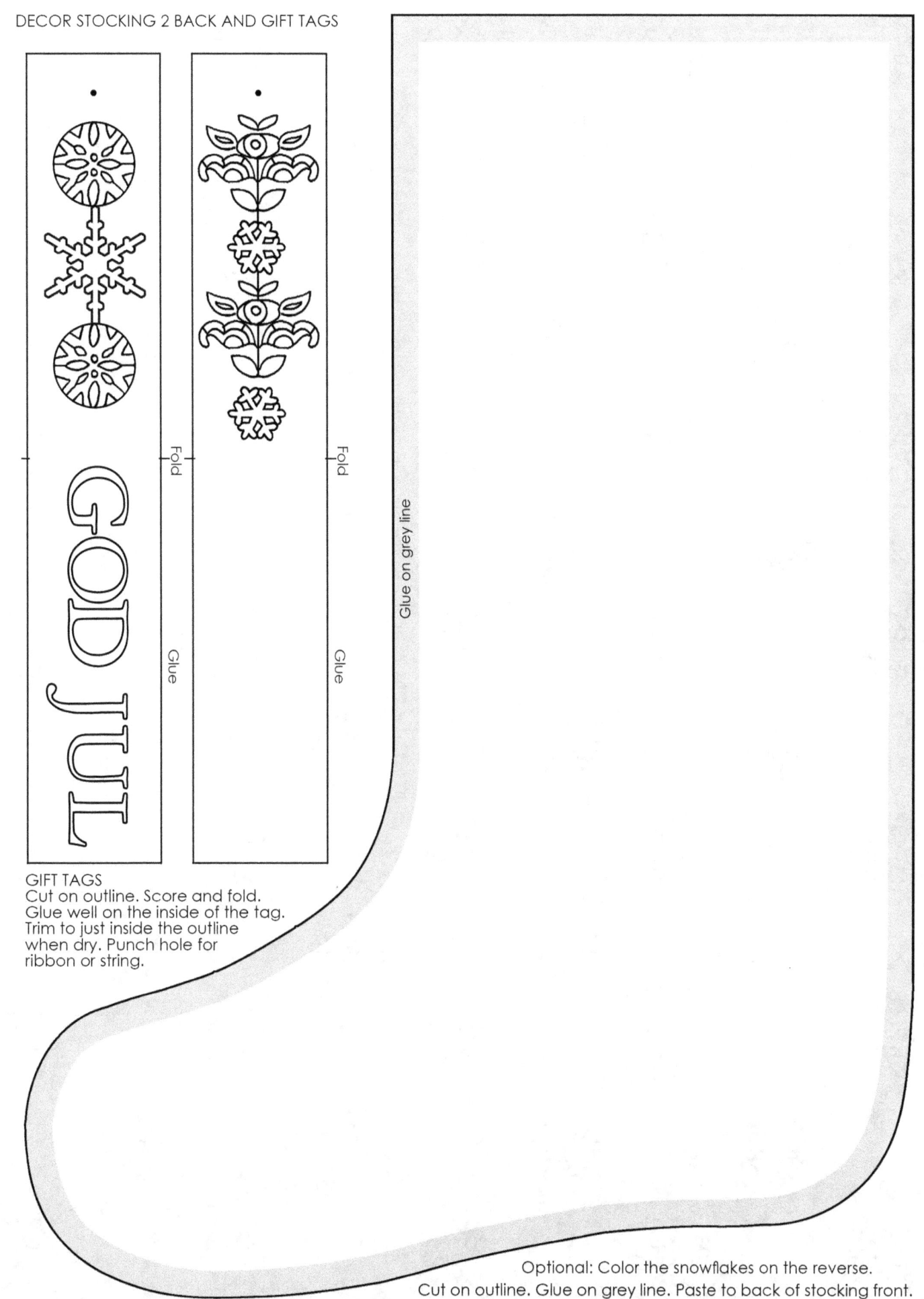

© ANNI ARTS

THE SCANDINAVIAN FOLK CHRISTMAS

Christmas traditions in Scandinavia reflect age-old pagan solstice festivals, shamanic practices and harvest festivals that were transferred to Christmas. The pagan word for solstice *"jul"* - or *"joulu"* in Finnish - has remained as the word for Christmas.

Straw truly reflects the spirit of the Scandinavian Christmas. The pagan solstice festival to celebrate the returning sun featured straw from the harvest as a symbol of the crops that were killed by winter, but that would grow again because of the sun's life-giving warmth. A goat was sacrificed as symbol of the slain god of winter. The goat was also the central figure in the straw-goat pageants that took place in autumn after threshing. The making of straw figurines and objects took place after straw-making and these were intended as amulets for protection. Red ribbons were often interwoven with the straw. The original straw-goat talisman became the popular Scandinavian *julbock* Christmas decoration when this event replaced the ancient solstice and harvest festivals. These days the straw *julbock* graces the Christmas table.

The word for Father Christmas is *"julbock"* or *"joulupukki"* in Finnish - which literally means Christmas goat and indicates that he was once associated with an animal figure, namely the straw-goat of the harvest festivals. During the harvest pageants a person was dressed in a goat costume with horns. The Christmas straw-goat took on a human form, but retained the animal name.

According to Christmas lore the St Nicholas tradition played a role in the humanisation of the goat. However, there are once again very ancient and forgotten Scandinavian pagan traditions that were amalgamated into a new version. The chief druid wore a red garb trimmed with white edgings, and dispensed gifts at solstice. The gifts were often in the form of entheogen mushrooms like the *Amanita muscaria* fairy tale mushrooms. These fly agaric mushrooms induce a euphoric feeling of flying on a shamanic journey. Reindeer too, love to eat the mushrooms – hence the lore of flying reindeer by association. So the red and white robed Father Christmas figure and flying reindeer are all firmly rooted in the very ancient North!

The modern day custom of the decorated Christmas tree was imported from Germany, but this essentially was a re-awakening of the ancient traditions in Scandinavia associated with the sacred evergreen tree. There are also links with hallowed tree groves and the mythical Yggdrasil. Folkloric customs of decorating the house and yard with birch and rowan branches at Midsummer and the name day fir tree allude to the importance of sacred trees in the Northern countries.

The Christmas troll or *"tomte"* or *"nisse"* goes back to beliefs in gnomes living underground, as well as to earth spirits. The household troll was largely responsible for the family's welfare and was believed to reside in the threshing barn. He had to be wooed and pacified and the custom of taking him a plate of porridge on Christmas Eve was a gesture of thanks for his generosity. Modern Christmas trolls are Scandinavian children that wear red outfits and red pointed hats.

The tradition of the Christmas ham goes back to the roasted wild boar of the *jul* fests. In earliest times the alcoholic beverage at celebrations was mead. Later, beer that was made from grain, as well as porridge and bread were important *jul* foods. The traditional Christmas bread has a sprig each of rye, wheat and oats from the autumn harvest that are stuck into the loaf as decoration.

Christmas in Scandinavia is celebrated on the 24th on Christmas Eve. *Jul* brings warmth, joy and light to the darkest time of year in the North. *God jul!*

(I did the Anni Arts illustrations for these crafts in watercolors in the style of the painted Scandinavian folk toy horses and extended the look to an elk, reindeer, julbock, tree and my own version of the painted toy horse. I used my original pencil drawings to do the line art for the Color and Craft Book)

EQUIPMENT
Only a few basic items are needed to make these creative paper crafts for Easter.

PENCIL CRAYONS, MARKERS or COLORED BALL POINT PENS
SCISSORS
CRAFT KNIFE with a sharp blade to cut straight lines (optional)
RULER (With a metal edge if used with a craft knife)
GLUE STICK
ADHESIVE TAPE (Use as an alternative to glue on some items.)
If you use tape, double-sided tape will be preferable as it can be concealed between layers.
PAPER SCORER
The bunting flags and tags have lines to be scored and folded.

A paper scorer is an instrument to draw a line to make folding that line easier.
It makes a dent on the card or paper, but does not cut right through. It is essential for creating tidy and precise paper crafts. Craft shops sell special scoring instruments, but an empty ballpoint pen is just as efficient – and is my personal favorite! You can also use the blunt side of the blade of a craft knife to make a *very light* score. And in a pinch you can also use a butter knife (with no serrations on the blade).
Note: When scoring regular paper like that used in this paper craft book, take care to score lightly – the paper can easily tear if the score runs too deep.

TIPS AND GENERAL INSTRUCTIONS
All pages have the relevant instructions printed with the paper craft item.

TIPS
First cut each craft page from the book along the guide line. A craft knife is handy for this.
The pictures for framing are in a ruled box and do not have guide lines
Color before cutting and making the Frame Art, Cards, Bunting, Decorations and Stockings.
(Or first cut a rough shape around the crafts and cards, do the coloring and then tidy the shape by cutting on the outlines.) The animals on the art pages can also be shape-cut when they have been colored and then glued to a patterned base. A red-and-white gingham page is included in the free downloads.
Anni Arts *https://www.anniarts.com/scandi-clip-art.html*
Score all lines as indicated, fold on the scored lines and glue or assemble as indicated.

GREETING CARDS
Make sure that glue goes all the way to the edges of the card elements. Lay a blank piece of paper over a freshly positioned and glued element and glide the edge of a ruler over the covered section to flatten and properly glue the element to the underlying layer. The cover paper protects the coloring and the glued elements.

The topper patches are glued to blank cards cut from cardstock.
Cut card bases to the dimensions given below, *or download the printable blank templates from Anni Arts* and print the card bases on printable cardstock at the link below. The card toppers can also be glued to postcards on a single card layer. The cards need purchased envelopes.
Anni Arts *https://www.anniarts.com/scandi-clip-art.html*

Cut a **10" x 7" (approx. 25.5 x 17.75 cm)** backing for a card that folds to **5" x 7"** (or cut a 5" x 7" postcard)
Cut a **8" x 6" (approx. 20 x 15 cm)** backing for a card that folds to **4" x 6"** (or cut a 4" x 6" postcard)
Score through the middle to fold the card and add the card making elements to the front.

www.ingramcontent.com/pod-product-compliance
Lightning Source LLC
LaVergne TN
LVHW062001070526
838199LV00060B/4231

9789527268179